God Don't Make JUNK

By
Michelle Knight

Illustrated by
Benedicta Buatsie

Editor: Carla M. Dean of U Can Mark My Word, LLC.

Illustrator: Benedicta Buatsie

ISBN:
Softback: 978-1956911-14-5
Hardback: 978-1956911-13-8

God Don't Make Junk

It was a beautiful summer day with not a cloud in sight, a perfect day for an afternoon in the park, and that's exactly what Kristie and her mom decided to do--walk to the nearby playground and enjoy a day under the sun.

When Kristie and her mom reached the playground, Kristie skipped merrily to the swing set, excited to pump her legs and swing high into the sky.

4

Suddenly, she spotted a few kids sitting on a blanket and painting on canvases. Their drawings were beautiful! Kristie watched as they painted with confidence and ease, creating colorful flowers, life-like characters, and lovely cityscapes. Kristie took a seat on the empty swing and began swinging slowly as small tears formed in the corners of her eyes.

5

7

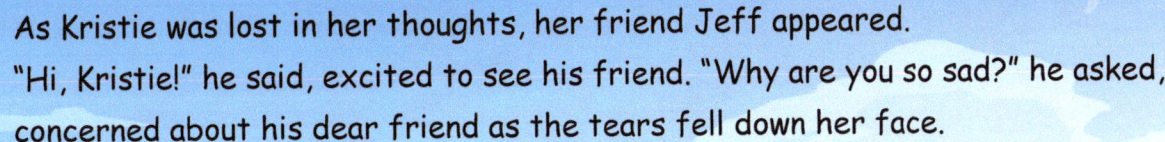

As Kristie was lost in her thoughts, her friend Jeff appeared.
"Hi, Kristie!" he said, excited to see his friend. "Why are you so sad?" he asked, concerned about his dear friend as the tears fell down her face.

"Hi, Jeff," Kristie replied in between sobs.
"I'm feeling down," she told him.

"I know how to cheer you up! Let's go feed the ducks by the pond!" Jeff said, full of excitement. "You love doing that," he added, remembering it was one of Kristie's favorite pastimes.

"No, not today, Jeff," Kristie replied, shaking her head. "Even the birds have talent, unlike me."

"What are you talking about?" Jeff asked, confused by Kristie's comment.

"Do you see those girls over there?" Kristie asked. "The ones sitting on the red blanket and painting? They're so talented! Then there's me, and I don't know how to do anything!" Kristie cried. "Jeff, you know how to play football and basketball, and Jessica knows how to dance. All our friends have talent except me. I feel awful."

10

11

"Kristie, please don't say that," Jeff said softly, trying to comfort his friend. "I'm sure you're good at something, and I will help you figure out what that is."

"Really?" Kristie said, wiping her tears as a smile formed on her face.

"Sure! That's what friends are for. Plus, my grandmother always taught me that 'God don't make junk.' Grandma has told me this for as long as I can remember, and I always keep her advice close to my heart. She taught me that everyone is good at something, and I believe that!" exclaimed Jeff. "You just have to figure out what interests you and allow God to let it grow."

"That's great advice, Jeff! *God don't make junk.* I like that. It has a special ring to it," Kristie excitedly said, feeling more hopeful.

"So, what do you want to try first?" Jeff asked.

Kristie and Jeff stood there for a moment, silently thinking about their next move.
"I know!" Jeff suddenly said. "Have you tried singing?"

Kristie paused and thought for a moment.

"No, not really," she replied. "Sometimes I sing along to the songs on the radio, but that's about it."

"Well, let's give it a shot! Maybe your hidden talent is singing," Jeff encouraged. "Repeat after me. La-la-la-laaaa!'" Jeff sang in his best voice, and it sure was nice.

Kristie cleared her throat, stood up straight, and began to sing.

"Laaaa!" she belted out.

However, her voice was not quite in tune and hardly easy on the ears.

14

Jeff politely listened, wondering how to tell his friend that maybe singing wasn't her hidden talent.

"Kristie, let's explore another talent," he kindly suggested.

"Wait. Before we do that, how was my singing? How did I do?" Kristie asked, hopeful he liked her voice.

"Well… Kristie…" Jeff nervously shifted from side to side. "I'm not sure singing is for you, but I'm confident you have other talents," he said, trying to remain optimistic.

Kristie's smile quickly disappeared. She slumped her shoulders and put her head down.

"Don't worry, Kristie. Let's move on," Jeff kindly urged. "I know! Maybe you're a great chef!" he suggested.

16

Kristie nodded in excitement, and the two friends decided to go to Jeff's house to cook. Luckily, Jeff lived nearby, only a two-minute walk from the park.

Jeff's mom and Kristie's mom agreed to join the kids as they walked to Jeff's house to cook.

When Kristie set foot in the kitchen, she suddenly felt nervous.

"I-I-I don't know about this," she stammered.

"You won't know until you try," Jeff reminded her. "We'll start with something simple like eggs and toast. It's easy-peasy," he reassured his friend as he grabbed her an apron from the closet. "Once you feel comfortable whipping up this meal, you can begin cooking other items and exploring new cuisines! As for the eggs, all you have to do is crack each egg over a bowl, beat them with a fork, then add salt and pepper."

"Wait!" Kristie cried out. "You're going too fast. I've only eaten eggs and have never cooked them. This is a lot to remember."

Jeff chuckled. "Don't worry. I'll guide you and answer any questions you have. I've done this with my mom a million times."

With Jeff's mom's permission, the kids removed the ingredients from the refrigerator and began their quest to cook.

As Kristie removed the bread from the bread bag, Jeff turned to her and said, "I need to use the bathroom. Will you be okay until I get back?"

"I think I got it from here," Kristie told him.

As Jeff exited the kitchen, Kristie began beating the eggs in the bowl as Jeff instructed. Then, Kristie asked Jeff's mom to help her fry the eggs, which were now ready to cook.

After washing his hands, Jeff left the bathroom and ran back into the kitchen with excitement.
The kids giggled as they watched
Jeff's mom cook over the stove.

When the eggs were finished, Kristie helped Jeff's mom put them on a plate. Kristie sprinkled another pinch of salt and pepper over the eggs and paired her creation with a slice of toast and grape jelly.

"Your eggs are served!" Kristie announced as she placed the dish in front of Jeff.

"These eggs look great, Kristie! I'm ready to dig in," Jeff said as he prepared to take his first bite.
Crunch, crunch, crunch.

Jeff's face scrunched up in disgust as he reached for a napkin.

"Kristie...where did you put the eggshells?" Jeff slowly asked as he spit his food into the napkin.

"In the recipe, silly! Do you like it? It's my secret ingredient," Kristie stated proudly with her head held high.

"Kristie, you're supposed to crack the eggs into the bowl *without* the shells. I'm sorry, but I don't want to eat this," Jeff told her, trying to be polite.

Kristie's giant grin immediately turned into a frown.

"I ruined the eggs," she said sadly. "I doubt I'll ever figure out my talent."

"C'mon, Kristie. Cheer up. God don't make junk, remember?" Jeff said encouragingly.

The two friends walked to the living room to watch TV. A few minutes passed, and Kristie felt a bit restless. So, she moved to an open space in the room and began somersaulting.

Flip, flip, land.

Back and forth, she flipped, landing perfect somersaults.

With poise and grace, Kristie tumbled around in Jeff's spacious living room,
landing smoothly after each flip.

Jeff quietly watched as his friend continued to do some indoor gymnastics. Within minutes, Kristie had somersaulted, leaned into a backbend, and did a perfect handstand.

Kristie sure was flexible!

"Kristie, this is incredible!" Jeff shouted with glee.

Taken by surprise, Kristie looked at Jeff in confusion.

"What's incredible?" she asked.

"Your gymnastic skills!" he said. "You're a fantastic gymnast. Why didn't you tell me this before?"

"I just tumble for fun," Kristie replied as she continued flipping across the carpet. "I didn't think anything of it," she added with a shrug.

"You have a true talent, Kristie. Can you teach me to do a handstand?" Jeff asked, excited about his friend's newly-revealed skill.

"Of course, I will teach you," Kristie said with a giant grin. "That's the least I could do for you. After all, you taught me an important lesson––God don't make junk!"

Louisiana native, currently residing in Virginia. Author Michelle Knight is an Army Veteran, wife to a retired Marine, proud mother of three, and grandmother to one. Her educational background includes a Bachelor of Science in Psychology, and a Master of Science in Healthcare Administration. Dedicating over 20 years working within the healthcare field,

Author Knight believes the biggest degree one can have is life experience. Everyone's life is different, although life can deal a deck of cards full of jokers. Through trials and tribulations, Author Knight developed a passion to teach through writing, as well as creating multicultural messages within literacy. Hence her motto, "Reading Reality Is Essential, Assisting our children through today, for a better tomorrow."

Creating Black Moms Reality Bookcase allows Author Knight to continue to fulfill her purpose and mission by providing reading material with life lessons. Thin books can have a powerful message as well. Showcasing diverse reads, with teachable moments featuring our African American children.

Other Works:

"Curby the Cow"

"Shhh, Don't Tell"

"The Queen in my Eyes is Mommy"

"The Friendship Tree"

www.ingramcontent.com/pod-product-compliance
Lightning Source LLC
Chambersburg PA
CBHW041436120626
46547CB00002B/237